Lots of Birds

by Becca Houston

 HOUGHTON MIFFLIN HARCOURT
School Publishers

PHOTOGRAPHY CREDITS: Cover © Gary Carter/Corbis; Toc © William Leaman/Alamy; 2 © Gary Carter/Corbis; 3 © William Leaman/Alamy; 4 © Arthur Morris/CORBIS; 5 William Leaman/Alamy; 6 © Penny Boyd/Alamy

Printed in India

ISBN-13: 978-0-547-42655-6
ISBN-10: 0-547-42655-0

2 3 4 5 6 7 8 0940 18 17 16 15 14 13 12 11 10

What do **you** see?
I see a red bird.

What do you see?
I see a white bird.

What do you see?
I see a blue bird.

What do you see?
I see a yellow bird.

What do you see?
I see a green bird.

Responding

✔ **WORDS TO KNOW** **Word Builder**

Ask a question about the color of your favorite bird. Use the word "what" in your question.

✏️ **Talk About It**

Text to Self Ask your friends if they like red birds or blue birds. Use vocabulary words in your question.

WORDS TO KNOW

| what | you |

TARGET STRATEGY **Visualize**

Picture what is happening as you read.